Flying Saucers, Rockets and Spaceships

Nick Robinson

CAXTON EDITIONS

First published in the UK in 1999 by
Caxton Editions
16 Connaught Street
Marble Arch
London W2 2AF

Copyright © Mars Publishing 1999

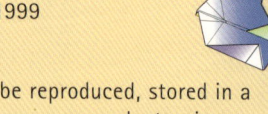

All rights reserved. No part of this publication may be reproduced, stored in a retrieval system or transmitted, in any form or by any means, electronic or mechanical, including photocopying, recording or otherwise, without the prior written permission of the copyright owner and publisher.

ISBN: 1-84067-093-2

This is a MARS book

Edited, designed and produced by Haldane Mason, London

Acknowledgements

Art Director: Ron Samuels

Editorial Director: Sydney Francis

Editor: Jane Ellis

Design: Zoë Mellors

Artwork: Nick Robinson

Printed in China

Photographs reproduced with kind permission of:
Jerry Schad/Science Photo Library **p. 4**; NASA/Science Photo Library **pp. 5, 7, 9, 13 and 20**; Tony Craddock/Science Photo Library **p. 11**; Columbia (Courtesy Kobal) **p. 15**; Warner Bros (Courtesy Kobal) **p. 16**; Twentieth Century Fox (Courtesy Kobal) **p. 18**

Every effort has been made to trace the copyright holders and we apologize in advance for any unintentional omissions. We would be pleased to insert the appropriate acknowledgement in any subsequent edition of this publication.

Contents

Introduction	4
A History of Rockets	6
How Rockets Work	8
UFOs	14
Table of Events	20
Making Your Spacecraft	22
Spacecraft Designs	26
• Escape Pod	28
• Space Seed	29
• Alien Lander	30
• Lunar Probe	32
• Space Shuttle	34
• Flying Saucer	36
• Mobile	38
• Plan 9	40
• Martian Bat (Male)	42
• Martian Bat (Female)	46
• Moon Scout	50
• Comet	54
• Star Fighter	58
Glossary	62
Index	63
Acknowledgements	64

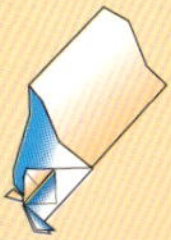

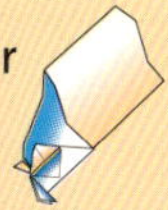

FLYING SAUCERS

Introduction

Since human beings first looked at the heavens, the vast emptiness of outer space has both fascinated and frightened them. Many early civilizations worshipped the Sun and Moon as gods, all powerful and ever-present.

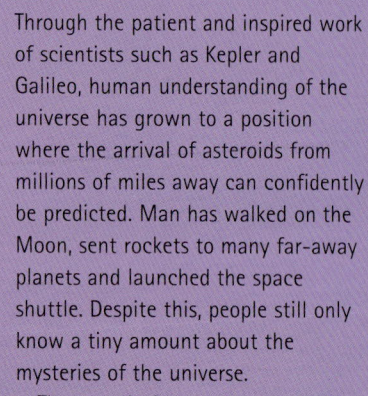

Through the patient and inspired work of scientists such as Kepler and Galileo, human understanding of the universe has grown to a position where the arrival of asteroids from millions of miles away can confidently be predicted. Man has walked on the Moon, sent rockets to many far-away planets and launched the space shuttle. Despite this, people still only know a tiny amount about the mysteries of the universe.

The appeal of outer space is that it gives us a better understanding of how the universe developed, how humans came to inhabit the Earth, and what might happen in millions of years time. The rate at which technology has progressed is amazing; less than 100 ago, science-fiction writers such as H.G. Wells wrote about spaceships and rockets that would enable man to travel from Earth to the Moon, Venus and Mars. Even 50 years ago this was still a dream. Nowadays, all that has been achieved, although these journeys are hugely expensive and there are only limited resources available.

The Milky Way, our own galaxy, seen over a line of trees. The large bright patch is the starcloud M24.

Eureca satellite being deployed from Shuttle Atlantis, 1 August 1992. Eureca carries out various experiments in life and materials science and radiobiology.

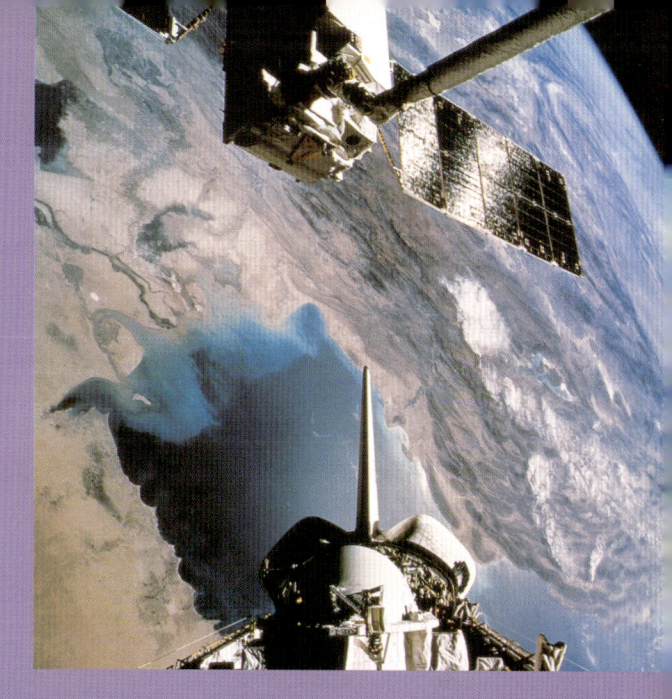

Rockets and space flight have also been responsible for the great improvement in communications around the world. Without satellites, all telephone and television signals would have to be sent along land-based cables, and the Internet would probably not have evolved.

As humans have learned to travel away from Earth, they have also become more aware that there may be other beings making the opposite journey. Stories of aliens and spaceships have intrigued thousands of people for many years and eventually it may be possible to prove their existence.

This book will explain the main principles behind space flight, as well as investigating the possibility that beings from other planets have been visiting the Earth for many years! You will be able to construct your own spaceships, rockets, alien craft and lunar landers. While they may not actually leave our atmosphere, using your imagination they could travel anywhere in the universe!

FLYING SAUCERS

A History of Rockets

The first people to use rockets were the Chinese, nearly 1,000 years ago. These rockets were powered by gunpowder and were not very accurate or reliable. In fact, they were rather like large fireworks. Nevertheless, they must have been a terrifying sight to the enemy!

The idea of travelling in space was a popular one amongst science-fiction writers such as Jules Verne, who wrote *From the Earth to the Moon* in the late 1800s. The first rockets to use liquid fuels successfully were designed and tested by the American Robert Goddard in the 1920s. Similar work was carried out in Germany by Werner Von Braun, whose work led to the two rocket-powered weapons of the Second World War, the V1 and V2.

The V2 was one of the most frightening of all the weapons designed by German scientists. At 15 metres, it carried a warhead of one tonne and had a range of about 288 kilometres. The engine thrust of 25 kilograms sent it far into the sky, from where it descended faster than the speed of sound to smash into the ground. Several of the scientists involved in German rocket technology were employed by the Americans after the war to assist with their own researches.

The Americans made many experiments with jet and rocket engines, breaking the sound barrier in 1947 and continuing to develop rockets that flew faster and higher. The Russians were also working towards

THE HISTORY OF ROCKETS AND AIRCRAFT

space travel and Yuri Gagarin became the world's first spaceman in 1961.

The rivalry between Russia and America led to rapid progress in space flight and only eight years after Gagarin, Neil Armstrong became the first man on the Moon. In less than 70 years, man had progressed from his first flight to walking on the Moon.

Space travel took a back seat for many years, partly due to the huge cost (the Apollo Project cost $24.5 billion!) and partly because space scientists realized they needed a more efficient way of leaving and returning to Earth. Many imaginative and unusual designs were produced, resulting in the first flight of the space shuttle in 1981.

This allowed the Americans to reuse much of the equipment needed to enter space and so keep the cost down.

...and the future?

With many people questioning the need for expensive space exploration while there is still so much poverty and hardship on Earth, governments have to limit the amount of money they can spend on new projects. The shuttle is currently taking parts into orbit to be assembled into a large space station (it will be visible without a telescope!) and this will allow space technologies, such as providing food and oxygen, to be put to the test and further developed. Spacecraft have landed on Mars and this may be the next target for a manned flight. The main problem is the distance; Mars is 54 million kilometers away, which means that it would take a total of six years to travel there and back. The dilemma of providing enough food and oxygen for such a journey has yet to be solved.

Astronaut Duke taking samples of lunar soil during the Apollo 16 mission, April 1972. The visit lasted 71 hours and the astronauts covered 26 kilometres in their Lunar Roving Vehicle (far left).

FLYING SAUCERS

How Rockets Work

Aircraft need air to fly. They are forced forwards by propellers or jet engines that provide thrust. The shape of their wings is designed to slice through the air in such a way that the pressure of air is higher underneath the wing, providing lift. As well as lift, the air pressure is used to control the aircraft in flight. It is also a vital ingredient in the engines; all types of aircraft engines need oxygen to work.

The density of air is greatest at sea level and gets lower as you go upwards. At eight kilometres up, it is about one quarter as dense, meaning that there is less lift, less control over the flight and the engines are not as efficient. At 32 kilometres up, there isn't enough air to keep the aircraft flying. This height is known as the 'absolute ceiling' and explains why we can't fly ordinary aircraft into outer space.

To climb a stair, you press your feet downwards. To climb a rope, you pull your hands downwards. These are examples of an important law of physics: to move in a given direction, you must exert a force in the opposite direction. This is Newton's Third Law of Motion: 'to every action there is an equal and opposite reaction'. If you fire a gun, your arm is kicked backwards. If you pointed the gun at the floor and fired, the recoil would force the gun into the air. A rocket works in a similar way, except instead of a bullet, a stream of hot gas fires downwards, forcing the rocket into the air. Since the stream of gas is continuous, the rocket keeps rising, provided the force is enough to overcome the weight of the rocket and the fuel. This is Newton's Third Law in action.

HOW ROCKETS WORK

The launch of Saturn V rocket on Apollo 9 mission, 3 March 1969.

The fuel is known as propellant (because it propels the rocket) and when lit, it burns to make combustion gases. These gases expand very quickly to produce enormous pressure. By making a small opening at one end of the chamber in which the gases burn, the pressure is all in one direction. Unlike early rockets that were powered by gunpowder, liquid-fuel rockets can control their speed by pumping more or less fuel into the combustion chamber.

The propellants need large storage tanks, since a rocket needs a great deal of energy to launch it. However, once the fuel has been burned, the tanks are not needed. They are then ejected or 'jettisoned' during the time when the rocket is leaving the atmosphere. As the rocket is launched, it meets air resistance (known as drag) so the design of the rocket and the fuel tanks is kept long and thin, enabling them to cut through the air with as little effort as possible. They also have to be lightweight, since more weight needs more fuel and this creates more weight! Rockets must also be able to withstand the intense heat created by the burning fuel in the combustion chamber. Even with modern heat-resistant metals, some form of cooling is still necessary, so as well as the propellant, all rockets require large tanks of coolant.

Escape velocity

To leave the ground, any kind of flying device needs energy to overcome the force of gravity. Balloons use lighter-than-air gas, aircraft use their engines, and rockets use the power of explosive gases. Modern spacecraft consist of two sections: the rocket which provides enough thrust to leave the atmosphere

FLYING SAUCERS

and the part that is actually being launched, known as the 'payload'. This load may be astronauts or perhaps a satellite being launched into orbit.

If a rocket is to leave the Earth's atmosphere, it needs to climb at 11 kilometres a second, a speed known as 'escape velocity'. To launch a rocket at this speed requires enormous power, especially when the weight of the fuel and the rocket itself is added to that of the payload. The NASA space shuttle uses a huge launching rocket to achieve escape velocity. Once it has reached space, it disengages and continues under its own power.

Early flights into space, such as the Apollo Missions, consisted of three-stage rockets. The first stage provided the initial thrust to reach the edges of the atmosphere, then fell back to Earth. The second stage took over and powered the rocket out into space. This section too fell away and was burned up as it re-entered the atmosphere. The final payload continued into space with only tiny rockets used for guidance.

In space, the effects of gravity disappear, as well as all effects caused by air pressure (such as lift and drag). This makes it difficult to control movement. Objects pushed in one direction would keep moving in that direction forever or until they drifted into the gravitational pull of a planet or asteroid. Rockets are only needed to reach the escape velocity, when they can be turned off without loss of speed. Once the craft has reached the required speed, small thrusters are used to change the direction of travel, since the control surfaces of an aircraft (rudders, ailerons, etc.) don't operate in the airless environment.

How do they stop?

Having reached the speed needed to escape the Earth's atmosphere and travelled to its destination, the next problem is how the rocket is going to stop. Brakes, as used in a car, would have no effect in space because there is no friction to slow the rocket down. It will keep moving unless something either pushes against it or pulls it back. There are two approaches to this. One is to use small jets of gas which fire forwards (called 'retro rockets'). Released in small bursts, they will reduce the rocket's speed. Another way is to use small directional thrusters to turn the rocket completely round (so it is facing backwards), then use the main rocket to slow down.

HOW ROCKETS WORK

Saturn V rocket, the type used to launch the Apollo missions to the Moon. The rockets were 100 metres tall and were fuelled by liquid hydrogen.

Orbiting

When a satellite is launched into space, there are several possibilities. If the rocket doesn't have enough speed, it will fall back to Earth. If the speed is too great, it will travel away from the Earth and vanish into space. The rocket has to reach a speed where the satellite will go round the Earth in a circular orbit, keeping the same distance all the time. A speed of 29,000 kilometres per hour will produce an orbit of 320 kilometres above Earth. For a rocket to launch a satellite into orbit, complex calculations must be performed, involving the weight of the rocket, the desired height, the speed of the Earth's rotation, and the time of year. All orbiting satellites eventually fall to Earth where they will be burned up.

11

FLYING SAUCERS

Life in space

Astronauts in space have to work in zero gravity, where nothing appears to have any weight. Everyday acts such as eating and drinking become difficult without gravity. For example, the liquid may float out of a glass every time the astronaut tries to drink it! If an astronaut stands up, he will keep going until he hits the ceiling. Weightlessness can be counteracted by making the rocket spin as it flies. This creates a kind of artificial gravity, because floating objects are attracted to the outside wall. When circular space stations are built, these too will rotate to provide the effects of gravity.

Coming home

A spacecraft could work in space almost indefinitely, if powered by solar panels, but supplies of food, drink and oxygen are limited. This means every astronaut must return home within a short time. In the future, it may be possible to grow food in space and create oxygen, allowing for longer flights. Getting back to Earth is an important part of the flight. The main problem is that when objects enter the Earth's atmosphere, they heat up due to friction with the air. Most of the tiny asteroids that strike the Earth burn up before they have a chance to do any damage, although larger ones will get through.

The temperature of re-entry can be so great that ordinary metals would melt. The base of the space shuttle is specially designed to withstand the heat of re-entry and must enter the atmosphere at a specific angle. This angle is worked out to balance the friction and re-entry time so that it keeps the heat to a minimum. Early spacemen returned in a tiny capsule that came through the atmosphere using a heatproof section of the capsule to withstand the massive friction caused on re-entry. They would then use a set of parachutes to slow them down to a safe landing speed. American craft landed at sea, where helicopters and boats would track their return and pick them up. Russian craft landed on dry land, since early space research was a highly secretive race between the East and West. Nowadays, the space shuttle glides in to land rather like a conventional glider.

Amazing life in space – astronaut Leroy Chiao spacewalks in the opened cargo bay of the shuttle Endeavour *as it passes over Shark Bay, Australia, 17 January 1996.*

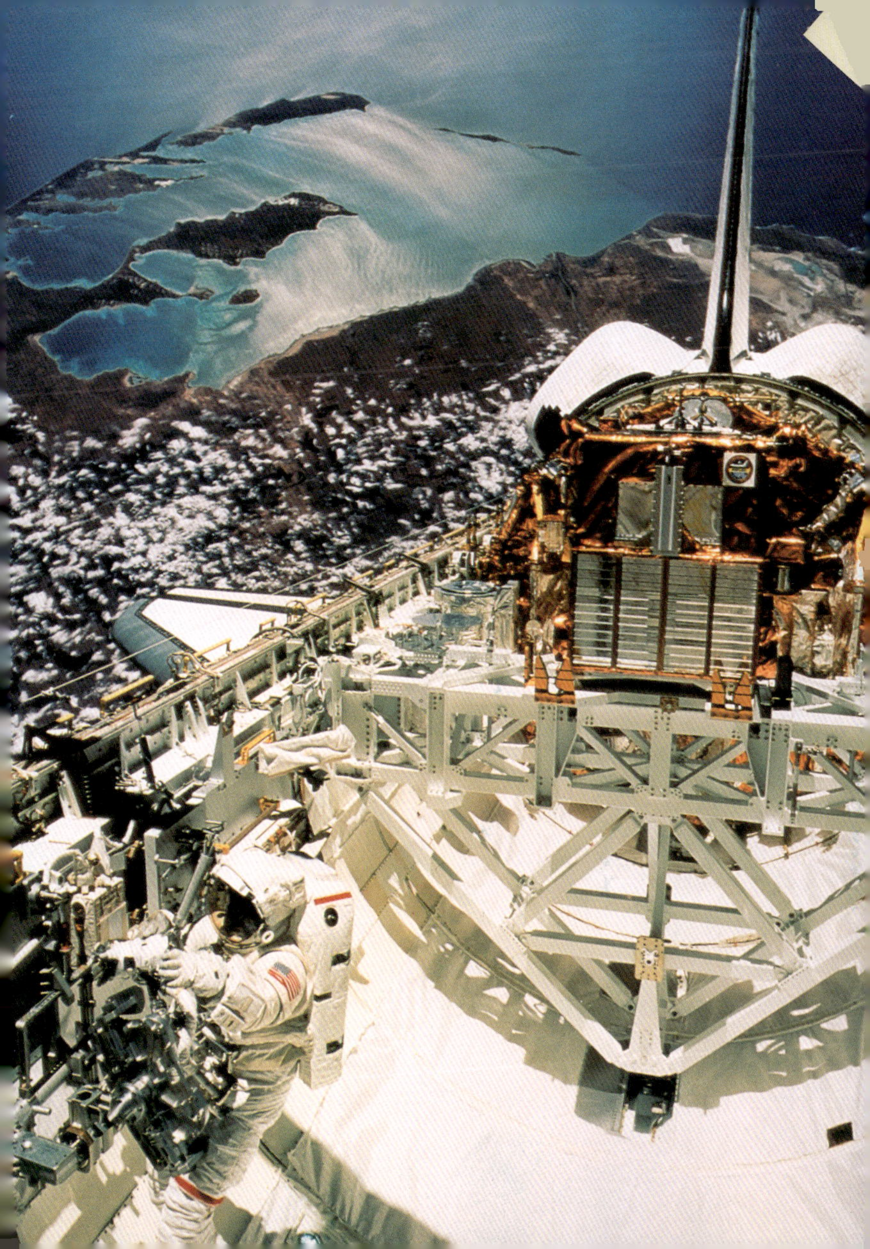

FLYING SAUCERS

UFOs

What does UFO mean? It is a name that covers all kinds of strange things that are seen in the sky. People don't know what they are, so they remain 'Unidentified'. They are in the sky so are 'Flying' and since we don't know what they are, we call them 'Objects'. People who claim to have seen a UFO are said to have had a close encounter of the first kind.

Is there any evidence?

Most of the reported sightings of flying saucers have taken place since 1947, but looking back through the ages, there have been many reports of bright lights and strange sights in the sky. There is even a reference in the Bible to seeing humanoid creatures with many heads, flying inside wheeled shapes. Some people believe that the pyramids in Egypt were built with alien help. In Mexico there are strange patterns carved in the rock which may have been landing plans for the spaceships of alien visitors. They were made over 1500 years ago!

During the Second World War, several American bomber crews reported strange glowing lights following their airplanes as they flew over Europe. They felt the lights were friendly and called them 'foo fighters'. There is no definite explanation for these and many similar stories. Lights of this kind may be caused by strange atmospheric effects, similar to the Northern Lights. Others may be caused by static electricity, odd-shaped clouds, car headlights behind a steep hill, weather balloons, bright planets, meteors, or even flying geese.

UFOs

Strange lights in the sky, from the 1977 film Close Encounters of the Third Kind.

FLYING SAUCERS

Evidence of UFO landings is virtually non-existent, since scorch marks and broken trees could be caused in many different ways. The fascinating crop circles that started to appear in otherwise untouched crop fields have been explained by alien landings. People who claim to have discovered real evidence of alien landings are said to have had a close encounter of the second kind.

Area 51 is a secret military air base about 150 kilometres north of Las Vegas, which the American Government refuses to talk about. The number 51 refers to the roughly 60-mile block of land that hides the base. The site was chosen in the mid-1950s for testing spy planes because it was quiet and a long way from populated areas, and it had a flat dry lake bed for take-offs and landings. Some people believe that Area 51 has become a place where the American Government is storing and hiding secret evidence that it has discovered about UFOs.

People who claim to have actually seen an alien face to face are said to have had a close encounter of the third kind. If you believe that there is intelligent life somewhere in the universe, then it seems likely that such a close encounter would take place at some time. After all, if a you were an alien who had flown across the galaxy to visit Earth in a spaceship, you would

What would aliens look like? This is how the 1997 film Mars Attacks! *portrayed them.*

UFOs

surely have wanted to get out and stretch your legs (all four of them!). A few people even believe that they have been kidnapped by aliens and taken aboard a flying saucer, back to the home world of the aliens. Explanations for what took place during these 'abductions' vary, from people claiming they have had experiments performed on them, to being made to breed with aliens. One suggested 'proof' of alien abduction is the existence of small electronic implants supposedly placed in the human subjects by alien doctors or machines. These may be listening devices or may have a more sinister purpose. It is impossible to say whether these stories are true or not, because some 'victims' can tell very convincing stories and can even pass lie detector tests. One explanation is that the wide variety of films, books and television programs about alien abduction cause people to have such vivid dreams that when they wake up they believe their dreams actually happened.

One of the most fascinating and controversial UFO stories is that of Roswell. In 1947 Colonel William Blanchard, an officer at Roswell Army Air Field, released the news that the wreckage of a crashed UFO had been

Site of Roswell in the USA.

found there. The story is that an alien spacecraft crashed near Roswell in the New Mexico desert, and that people who visited the site saw the bodies of aliens. When the military arrived they removed all traces of the wreckage and the aliens, then denied anything had happened! The story had died down for many years, but came back to life in a big way when film footage was released, apparently showing an alien being dissected by military doctors. Many people believe the film to be a hoax, created by special camera effects, but for a film over 50 years old, the effects are very convincing. Needless to say, the American Government has continued to deny any knowledge of an 'accident' at Roswell.

FLYING SAUCERS

Many films have been made about aliens invading the Earth. This still from Independence Day *(1996) shows a flying saucer attacking the White House, home of the American President.*

A more unpleasant UFO subject is that of cattle mutilations. All around the world, cattle have been found killed and totally drained of blood. There has been no trace of blood nearby, and sharp cuts have been found on the bodies, which appear to have been made by some kind of laser. Various parts of the bodies have been removed with medical precision and taken away. Since UFOs were allegedly seen at the same time and place of these attacks, the theory is that aliens carry out these horrible mutilations.

What is the truth behind all these stories? One problem in accepting that UFOs really exist is that human beings enjoy a good story. When a UFO

UFOs

sighting is reported in an area, there are usually many 'copy-cat' sightings in the same area over the next few months. Some people may actually believe they have seen a UFO, but others may simply want to impress their friends or to attract newspaper publicity for themselves. It is all too easy to get carried away by exciting stories. For example, in 1938 Orson Welles made a radio broadcast of *War of the Worlds*, a story by H.G. Wells about a Martian invasion of Earth. The acting and sound effects were so realistic that many thousands of listeners panicked and roamed the countryside with guns, looking for Martians!

Another reason for doubt is that with all these sightings of craft from outer space, none of them have left behind any evidence, such as alien paper, clothes, materials, or food. However advanced these aliens may be, it is likely they would have left something behind! Interestingly, in America people are forbidden to come into contact with a UFO or aliens under the ET (Extra Terrestrial) Exposure Law. If a person breaks this law, he or she can be fined up to $3,000 and be jailed for up to a year. The American Government apparently takes UFOs very seriously, despite denying their existence in public.

Photographs of UFOs are also easy to fake. All you need is an old hubcap or baking tray, someone to throw it, then take an out-of-focus picture with a camera. Expert photographers using computer software can also create images that are impossible to prove as fakes. Unfortunately, the more hoaxes that are discovered, the less chance there is that any real photographs of UFOs will be taken seriously.

FLYING SAUCERS

Table of Events

AD 900	The Chinese launch gunpowder-fuelled rockets.
1898	H.G. Wells writes *War of the Worlds*.
1902	The Russian Tsiolkovski proposes the ideas of liquid fuel and multi-stage rockets.
1903	Orville Wright makes the world's first powered, sustained, and controlled flight.
1923	*The Rocket into Interplanetary Space* published by Hermann Oberth in Germany.
1926	Robert Goddard launched the first liquid-powered rocket.
1932	Werner Von Braun (a student of Oberth's) starts work on liquid-propelled rockets in the army.
1935	Goddard launched the first rocket with gyroscopic controls.
1942	The first successful launch of Von Braun's V-2 missile.
1945	Von Braun and his team of 125 rocket scientists and

Robert Goddard beside the rocket that gave the first flight of a liquid propellant rocket in Massachusetts, USA, 16 March 1926.

TABLE OF EVENTS

	engineers surrender to the Americans to avoid execution by Hitler.
1947	With two broken ribs, Chuck Yeager became the first person to break the sound barrier, flying a Bell X-1.
1949	A V-2 boosted another rocket 393 kilometres into space at a speed of 8,867 kilometres per hour, the greatest altitude and velocity yet achieved by a man-made object.
1953	Yeager reaches Mach 2.5 in a Bell X-IA (two and a half times the speed of sound).
1954	Major Arthur Murray flew the X-1A to a record altitude of over 27,000 kilometres.
1957	The first satellite 'Sputnik' launched by Russians. Sputnik 2 launched with Laika the dog inside.
1961	Russian Yuri Gagarin becomes the first man in space.
1961	American President John F. Kennedy announces that America will land a man on the Moon before 1970.
1962	John Glenn makes the first American manned space flight in the Mercury space capsule.
1965	The first of the Gemini missions.
1965	Alexei Leonov makes the first 'walk' in space, fastened to Voshkod 2.
1968	Apollo 8 circles the Moon.
1969	Neil Armstrong is the first man to walk on the Moon as part of the Apollo 11 mission.
1971	Russia launches Salyut 1, the first space station.
1981	The first space shuttle is launched.
1984	Bruce McCandless makes the first 'unfastened' space walk.
1986	The space shuttle *Challenger* exploded 73 seconds after take-off, killing all seven astronauts.
1987	The Russians launch the Mir space station.
1990	The Ulysses Mission to study the solar wind via Jupiter.
1992	Mars Observer – NASA Mission to Mars.
1997	The Cassini Mission; NASA/European Space Agency trip to Saturn.
1999	Mars Polar Lander Mission to Mars.

FLYING SAUCERS

Making Your Spacecraft

Paper is one of the most simple materials to work with. It is cheap, available everywhere and comes in a huge range of colours and patterns. Most flying designs are made from rectangles, although some use a square. Photocopying paper is ideal and you can buy it very cheaply. If you keep your eyes open, you'll find plenty of free paper, such as adverts and leaflets that are pushed through your letterbox!

For flying designs, you should use fresh paper of medium weight. Thicker paper works, but might not fly very well if the model is too heavy. Thin paper can lose shape if you launch too quickly. Paper that has been left in the open for a long time can absorb moisture from the air and becomes 'floppy'. This prevents it from flying well. Cheaper types of paper, such as 'rice' or 'sugar' paper are OK for trial runs, but not for the real thing. Once you have mastered the folding method, you might want to look for some suitably patterned paper for a really special result. You can decorate it yourself with pencils and crayons. You could try using foil-backed paper for some of the alien designs.

MAKING YOUR OWN SPACECRAFT

To make a square from a rectangle

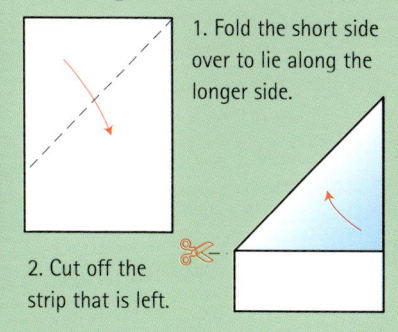

1. Fold the short side over to lie along the longer side.

2. Cut off the strip that is left.

Folding technique

When you start folding it's a good idea to use a table or other flat surface to fold on. If you are new to paper-folding, you should also stop between folds and look at the next diagram. Before creasing, check the paper is in the right place. If you get it wrong you can refold it, but the model won't fly as well with lots of wrong creases.

If you find it easier to make a fold by turning the paper around or upside down, do it, but don't forget to turn it back afterwards so that it matches the next diagram.

Using the instructions

The projects in this book are arranged with the easiest first, so it is suggested that you fold them in order. The diagrams show you a series of steps leading up to the finished spaceship. You must follow the instructions in the order shown! It's also useful to look ahead to the next step each time, so you know what you are aiming for. The first diagram will usually show creases already on the paper. These are always 'halfway' creases, made by folding the paper in half.

Symbols

Paper-folding is sometimes called by its Japanese name, 'origami'. People who practise origami have invented a set of standard symbols so that anyone can follow them, even if they don't speak the same language. The two basic creases are: a valley fold (indicated by a dotted line) and a mountain fold (indicated by alternating dots and

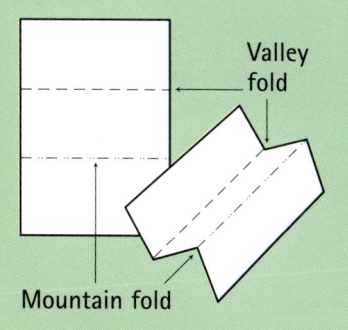

Valley fold

Mountain fold

23

FLYING SAUCERS

dashes). Other common symbols include 'pull the paper out', 'turn the paper over' and 'apply gentle pressure'. Once you become familiar with the symbols, you will be able to make origami designs from anywhere in the world.

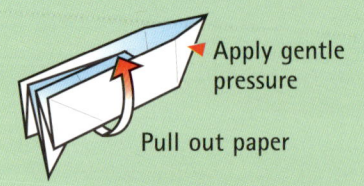

Apply gentle pressure

Pull out paper

Creating your own designs

The best way to create is to experiment with basic designs. Change the position of a crease and see how it affects the finished design. Add extra folds, miss folds out – you don't have to follow the diagrams! Keep an open mind – some quite unlikely looking designs fly extremely well. Your plane doesn't have to be a typical spaceship, it might be a new type of UFO or a stealth bomber.

Flight adjustments

There are three major factors that affect the flight of an alien craft or rocket; the angle of launch, the speed of launch and the angle of the wings.

Angle of launch

You can try launching your spacecraft in any direction from down at the floor to straight up in the air. In practice, each design will have an angle that gives the best results. Start by launching it forwards and slightly down; then note how it flies and try again with a slightly different angle. Try a wide range of angles to see which is best for your design.

Speed of launch

Some spacecraft fly best when launched slowly, others need a faster launch. Experiment to find the best.

Dihedral

A paper spacecraft is likely to turn in several different directions, but the biggest problem is often whether it rises or falls in the air. We can control this by adjusting the angle of the wings to each other, known as dihedral. The best dihedral is usually with the wings

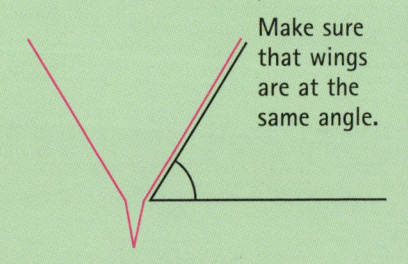

Make sure that wings are at the same angle.

MAKING YOUR OWN SPACECRAFT

pointing upwards slightly. As one wing lowers, the lift on the other wing reduces, causing the craft to move back to a more stable position. The angle of the wings will also vary for each design When altering the dihedral, always try to make sure both wings have the same angle, or it will roll.

As you might expect, the three factors affect each other. For example, if we increase the dihedral we may have to launch more slowly. After a while, you will learn to predict how this happens and adjust accordingly. Be patient and try to work out what is happening.

Fine tuning

Small changes to the back edge of the wings can have a large effect on the flight. Try to curl the tips of the wings slightly upwards. By deliberately making large curls, you can make craft perform spectacular aerobatics.

Weight

Some designs will work better from larger sheets, others best with small sheets. If the paper is too light, it will be blown too easily by the wind. If it's too heavy, it may not fly at all! The only way to find out is to experiment.

Height

Most flying designs work better if you launch them from higher up, such as a bedroom window. Make sure you don't attempt to launch yourself!

Top Ten Tips for folding paper spacecraft

1. Try to find somewhere quiet so you can concentrate.
2. Set aside 'folding time' so you won't feel rushed.
3. Use a table or flat surface to fold on.
4. Make sure your hands are clean.
5. Fold slowly and carefully, making sharp and accurate creases.
6. Look ahead to the next diagram to see what you're aiming for.
7. Try not to put in 'extra' creases – they will affect the flight.
8. Never launch your spacecraft towards anybody.
9. Don't give up if it doesn't fly properly.
10. Be prepared to experiment!

FLYING SAUCERS

SPACECRAFT DESIGNS

Spacecraft Designs

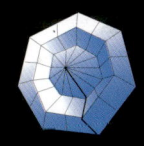

These exciting models range from simple designs such as the Escape Pod, to more complex craft such as the elegant Star Fighter. We have started with the easiest designs so that you get used to the techniques and following instructions. Soon you will feel confident enough to tackle even the most difficult spacecraft.

FLYING SAUCERS

Escape Pod

1. Start with an A4 sheet of paper. Cut a strip about 2 cm wide from one of the long edges.

2. About 3 cm in from the end, cut a slit no more than halfway across. Turn the paper round 180° and cut a matching slit on the opposite side.

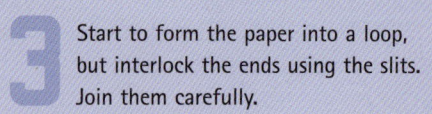

3. Start to form the paper into a loop, but interlock the ends using the slits. Join them carefully.

4. Your escape pod is ready for testing. Launch it as high into the air as you can, then watch it spiral safely to the ground. Smaller versions can be launched by blowing them from your hand.

Hints: try making the paper thinner or thicker and see what happens. Try making the slits nearer the end or the middle.

These are the emergency pods that aliens use when the UFO has been damaged or attacked. They fall out of an escape hatch underneath the UFO and spiral to safety.

SPACECRAFT DESIGNS

Space Seed

Traditional Design

Here is perhaps the simplest flying object you can make; one crease, two twists and a paper-clip! On Mars it is the equivalent of our sycamore seed. Hold it as high as you can and release gently.

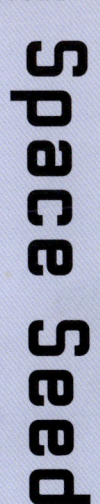

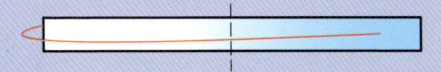

1 Using the method for the Escape Pod, start with a thin strip of paper (slightly thicker paper is best). Fold it in half.

2 Draw the paper across the edge of a ruler or table to curl the flaps outwards on either side.

3 Curl the flap around slightly – do not crease the paper. Repeat on the other flap.

4 Add a paper-clip and you are ready.

FLYING SAUCERS

Alien Lander

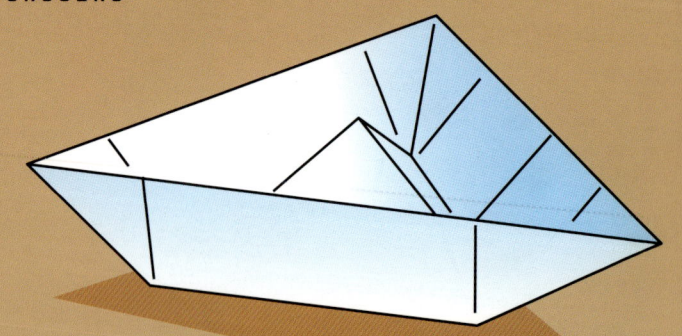

Design by John Smith

The Alien Lander is designed for safe re-entry into any kind of atmosphere. No matter which way you launch it, it will always turn the right way up and float safely to the ground. Ideal for close encounters of the third kind!

1 Start with a square that has both diagonal creases already made. Fold a corner to the opposite corners, but only crease to the centre.

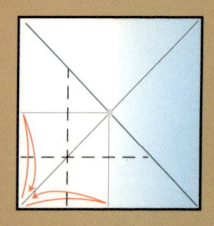

2 Turn the paper over and fold the same corner to the nearest halfway creases. This time, only crease up to the diagonals.

ALIEN LANDER

3 Add two more one-eighth creases, all the way across the paper.

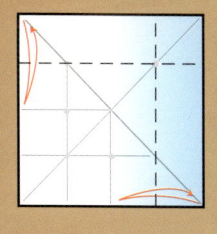

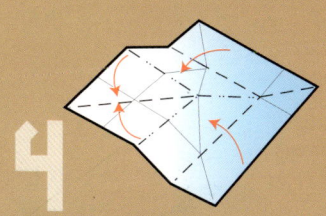

4 Make sure the creases match those shown here. Start to collapse the paper together ...

5 ... into this shape. Open out the nearest edge and look underneath the paper.

6 Fold the triangle in half, taking the tip of the corner to the centre of the paper.

7 Swing the smaller triangle upwards to lie flat.

8 Press in slightly from above, forming the sides of the lander. The centre section points upwards.

9 Turn the paper over for the completed Alien Lander.

31

FLYING SAUCERS

Lunar Probe

Design by Nick Robinson

This is a special type of top-secret probe launched by NASA in 1996. It was designed to land on the Moon, then rotate into the lunar surface to analyze the minerals. It needs to be launched from high up, so it can gather rotational energy during flight.

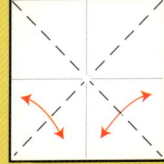

1 Start with a square that has been creased in half both ways. From the white side, add both diagonals.

2 Fold two opposite sides into the centre, crease and unfold.

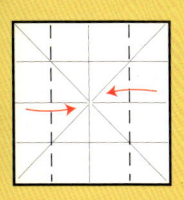

LUNAR PROBE

3 Fold the other two sides into the centre, then turn the paper over.

4 Using the creases shown, collapse the paper towards you. A similar move occurs in step 3 of the male Martian Bat.

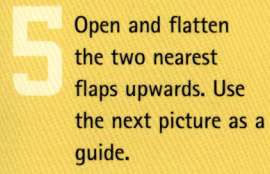

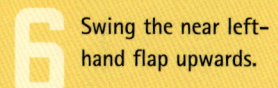

5 Open and flatten the two nearest flaps upwards. Use the next picture as a guide.

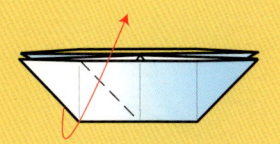

6 Swing the near left-hand flap upwards.

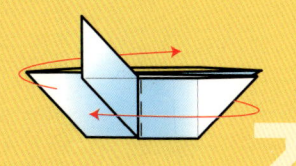

7 Fold the near right-hand flap to the left, then swing the lower left-hand flap behind to the right. It's easier than it sounds!

8 Repeat steps 6 and 7 with the other three flaps.

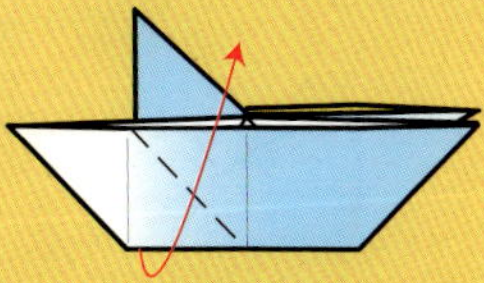

9 Move the flaps so that they are 90° apart from each other. Let the flaps open slightly and launch.

33

FLYING SAUCERS

Space Shuttle

Design by Nick Robinson

While not a flying model, this space shuttle design is superb as part of a mobile, where the valiant shuttles of Earth are sent up to keep away the massed ranks of flying saucers! The saucer design will fly if made from reasonably heavy paper. Make several models, then attach them to a mobile as shown on page 38.

Shuttle

1 Start with a square that has a diagonal crease. Fold one end of this crease to the other.

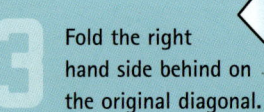

2 Fold both outer corners to meet the upper corner.

3 Fold the right hand side behind on the original diagonal.

SPACE SHUTTLE

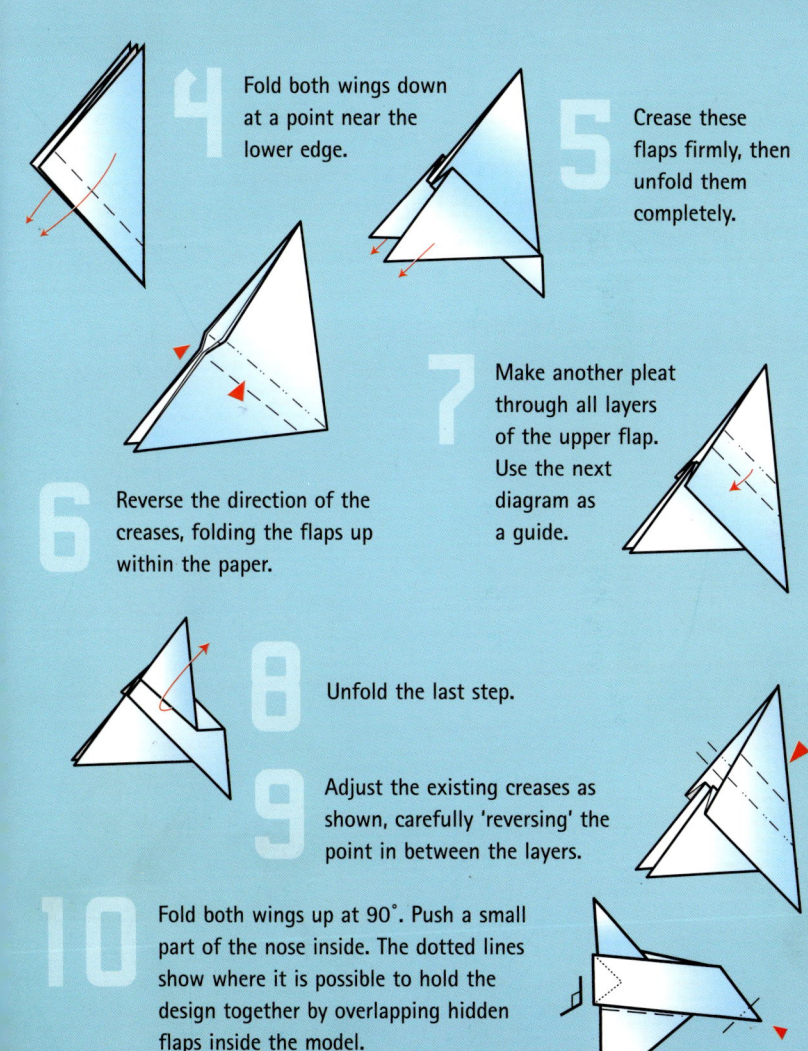

4 Fold both wings down at a point near the lower edge.

5 Crease these flaps firmly, then unfold them completely.

6 Reverse the direction of the creases, folding the flaps up within the paper.

7 Make another pleat through all layers of the upper flap. Use the next diagram as a guide.

8 Unfold the last step.

9 Adjust the existing creases as shown, carefully 'reversing' the point in between the layers.

10 Fold both wings up at 90°. Push a small part of the nose inside. The dotted lines show where it is possible to hold the design together by overlapping hidden flaps inside the model.

35

FLYING SAUCERS

Flying Saucer

Design by Nick Robinson

Here is the classic saucer, star of many science-fiction films in the 1950s. The model flies if you make it from heavy paper and give it a good spin, but is designed to be part of the mobile.

1 Start with the preliminary base (step 4 of the Moon Scout, page 51). Turn so the four original corners are towards you, then lift the upper left-hand flap and squash it evenly to either side.

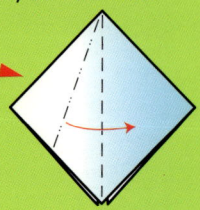

2 Like this. Repeat with the three other flaps.

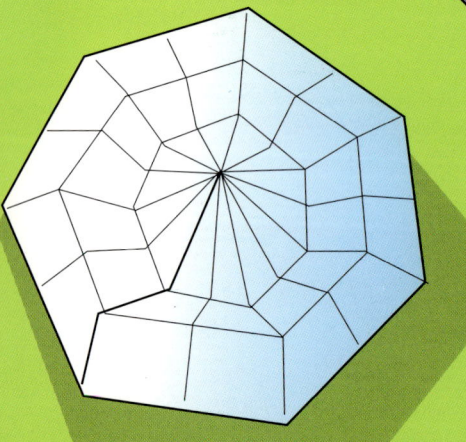

3 Fold the small triangular flaps over the coloured edge. Crease firmly and unfold. Repeat with the two flaps behind. Unfold the paper back to a square.

36

FLYING SAUCER

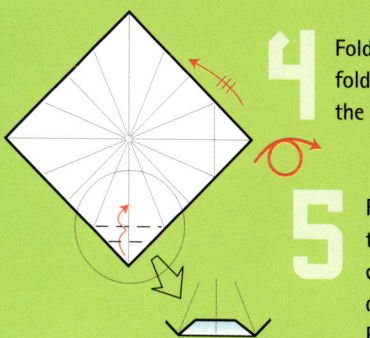

4 Fold a corner to meet the first crease, then fold over again using that crease. Repeat on the three other flaps and turn the paper over.

5 Fold an outside edge to the centre, but only crease between two diagonals, as shown. Repeat this move on all eight edges, then turn the paper over.

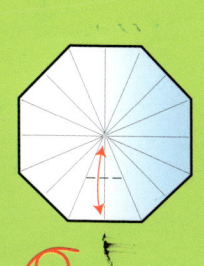

6 Fold the edge to meet the most recent crease, again creasing only where shown. Repeat this move on all eight edges.

7 Use the two creases shown to form the paper into three dimensions. The edges come towards you, the centre moves away from you.

8 Fold the short edge of the thick flap to the diagonal, then fold over again using the diagonal. The flap tucks under the small coloured section.

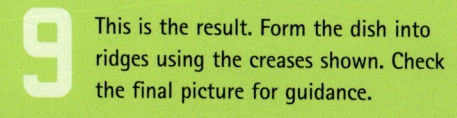

9 This is the result. Form the dish into ridges using the creases shown. Check the final picture for guidance.

37

FLYING SAUCERS

Mobile

To make an exciting action mobile to hang on your bedroom ceiling, this is what you need:

- two shuttles and two flying saucers
- one long mobile wire or rod
- two short mobile wires or rods
- seven lengths of thread, of varied lengths.

1 Use the wire to poke a small hole through the centre of the model, then pass the thread through it. To hold it in place, you can either tie a bulky knot on the thread, or fasten some sticky tape around the end. Hanging the model from a point slightly away from the centre will make it tilt and look more realistic. When you have tied the thread to the ends of the wires, cut away any loose ends to make a neat finish.

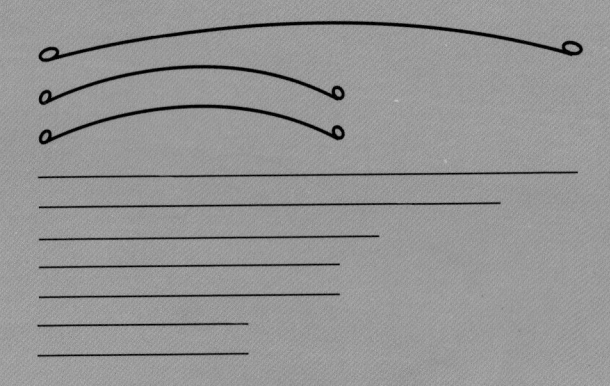

MOBILE

2 For each extra two models, you need an extra wire and three threads. Single extra models can be hung from the middle of a wire. You should arrange the models so they can rotate right round without touching the other models. This make take a little time, but is well worth the effort.

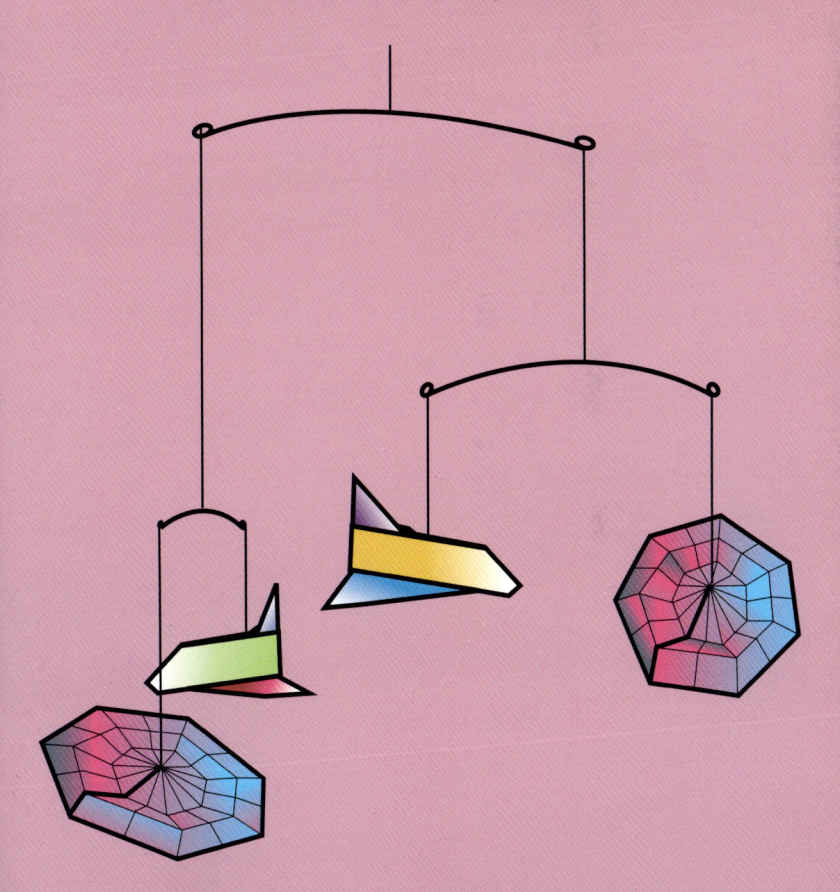

FLYING SAUCERS

Plan 9

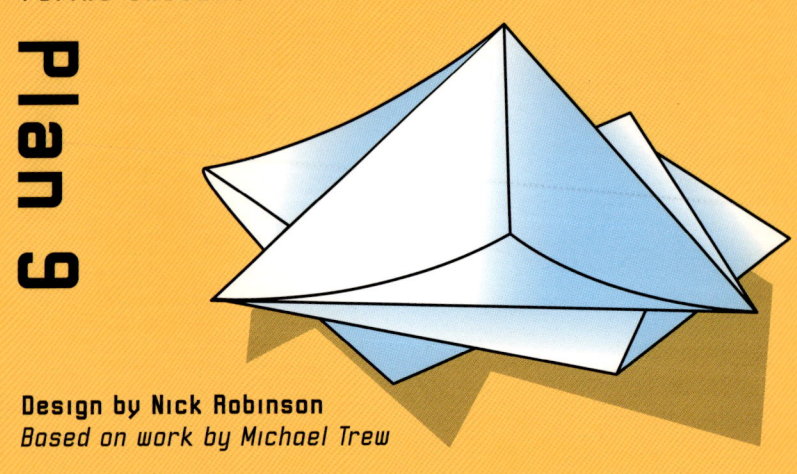

Design by Nick Robinson
Based on work by Michael Trew

Plan 9 from Outer Space is the title of a classic science-fiction film from the 1950s and inspired this design. The unusual sequence of twists results in a very solid model which, with a flick of the wrist, will spin on a table.

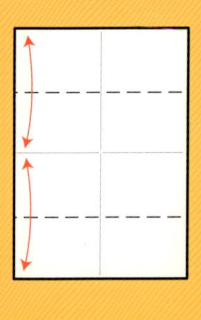

1 Start with a rectangle that has been folded in half both ways. Fold both short edges to the centre, crease and unfold.

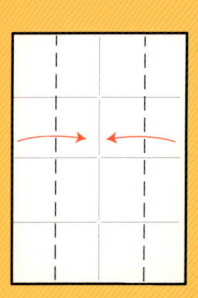

2 Now fold the long edges to the centre, crease and unfold. Turn the paper over.

PLAN 9

3 Carefully add diagonal creases as shown. If you make them accurate, the model will be easier to complete.

4 Turn the paper back over and fold on the valley creases. As the two ends start to meet, tuck one fully inside the other. You may need to open the paper a little to do this.

5 Using the creases made in step 3, begin to twist the left-hand half of the model. It may help to put your fingers inside the other half to keep the paper in shape. When the paper is fully twisted, it will form a slightly rounded dome.

6 Repeat the move on the other half. This time, the paper pushes inside the top half as the model is completed. Press all edges to reinforce the shape.

FLYING SAUCERS

Martian Bat (male)

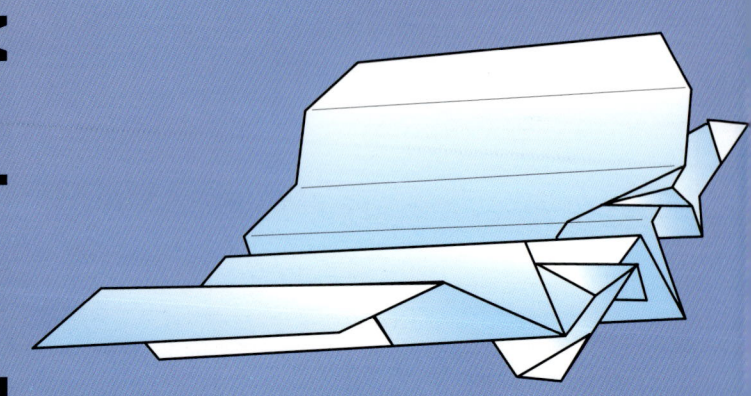

Design by Nick Robinson

The Martian atmosphere is much thinner than here on Earth, so the bats have evolved large gliding wings. They cannot make sudden movements and so are easy prey for the more mobile inhabitants of the Martian airways. The male has a much larger head than the female.

1 Start with an A4 rectangle, creased in half along the centre. Fold the top edge to meet one of the longer sides. Unfold and repeat to the other side.

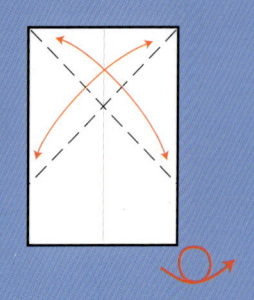

MARTIAN BAT (MALE)

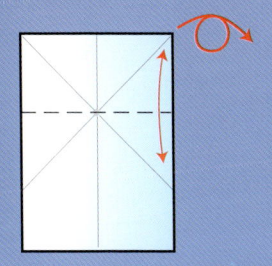

2 Turn the paper over and fold the top corners to meet the ends of the diagonal creases. Crease firmly and unfold again. Turn the paper over again.

3 Use all the creases shown to collapse the paper into a triangular shape with a loose point on either side. This is the starting point for many designs.

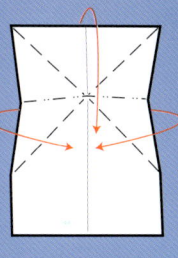

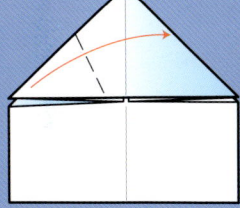

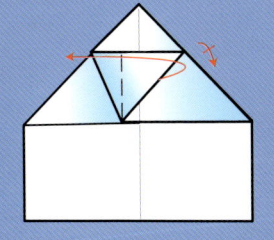

4 Fold the left-hand point across to touch the right hand edge, so that the top edge of the folded flap is horizontal. Check the next picture as a guide.

5 Now fold the same flap back on itself, starting at the lower corner of the flap. Repeat the last two steps on the other point.

FLYING SAUCERS

6 This is the result. Open up the first layer of the triangle a little way. The circled section is enlarged.

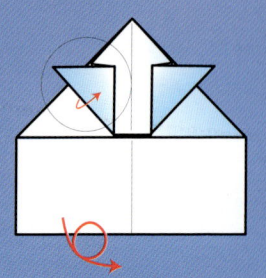

7 Fold the tip of the point back on itself to show some of the underside.

Refold the flap back to the left.

8 Like this. Repeat with the other flap.

9 Turn the paper over and fold the top corner to meet the middle of (hidden) layer underneath. You need to flatten two small flaps as this happens; use the next picture as a guide.

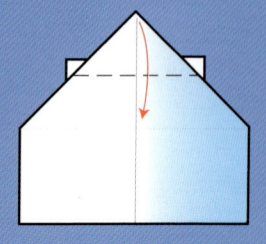

MARTIAN BAT (MALE)

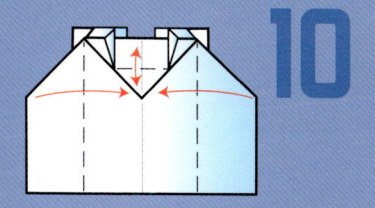

10 Fold the inside corner to the top edge, crease and unfold. Advanced folders can use this crease to 'lock' the design together once complete. Fold the left and right sides to the vertical centre crease.

11 Fold the outside edges to the centre, crease and unfold. Then open both wings.

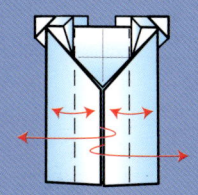

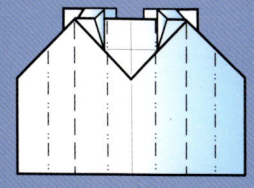

12 Change the creases where necessary to match this pattern. None of the creases opens fully, but form a 'stair' pattern as with the final picture.

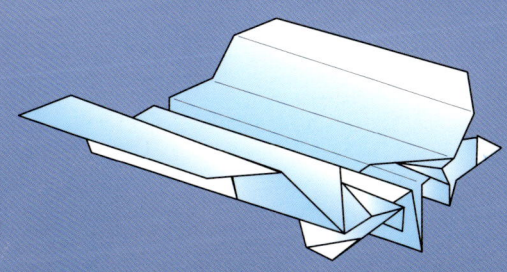

45

FLYING SAUCERS

Martian Bat (female)

Design by Nick Robinson

As with the male Martian Bat, the female has large gliding wings. Since she has to protect the nest, the female has large eyes to spot predators and sharp fangs to defend herself with. Careful adjustment of the wings will produce a slow, steady flight.

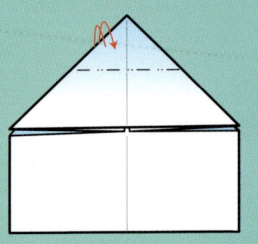

1 Start with an A4 rectangle, folded up to step 4 of the male Martian Bat. Fold the top triangle in half behind. Turn over and make a valley crease.

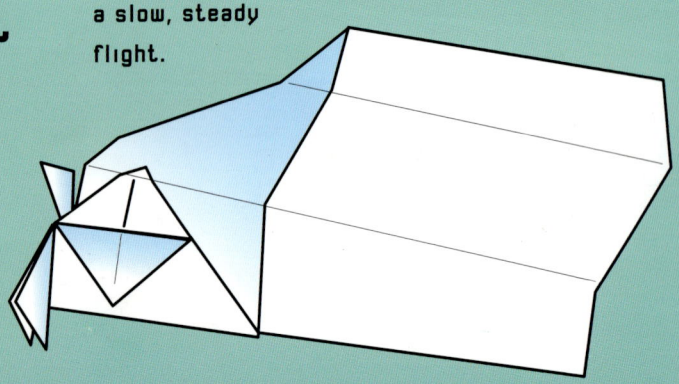

MARTIAN BAT (FEMALE)

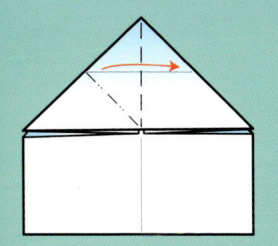

2 Fold the left-hand flap over to the right, then in half to the top corner.

3 Fold the same corner down, then out to the right.

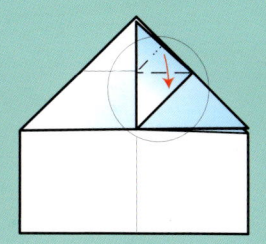

4 The circled area is enlarged here. Lift and squash the small triangular flap open.

5 Tuck half of the top layer inside.

6 This is the result, which forms the eye.

47

FLYING SAUCERS

7 Pull the flap back to the left.

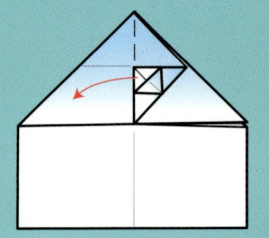

8 Make a small crease by taking to the outside edge to the vertical crease and back.

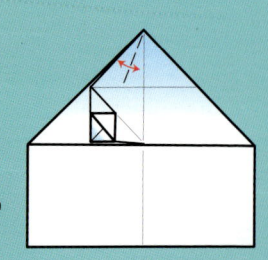

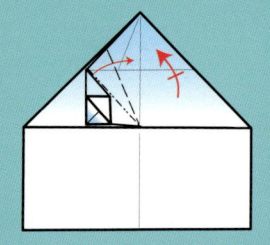

9 Swing the folded edge by the eye to meet the vertical crease. Repeat steps 2–9 on the right-hand side.

10 Fold the top corner behind using the creases shown. This is easier than it looks! Turn the paper over.

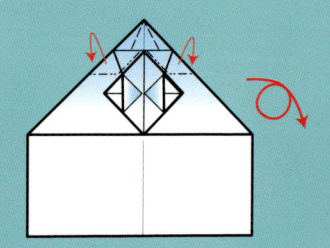

48

MARTIAN BAT (FEMALE)

11 Fold the model in half to the right.

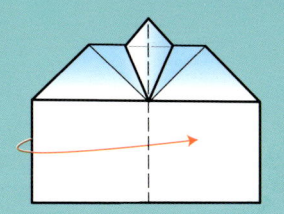

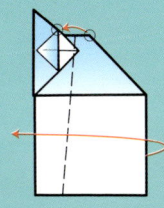

12 Form the wings by making the circled corners meet. The crease you make is not vertical.

13 Form vertical stabilizers by folding the outside edges to meet the hidden edge formed in step 11. Form both fangs.

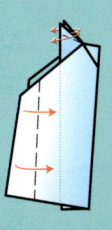

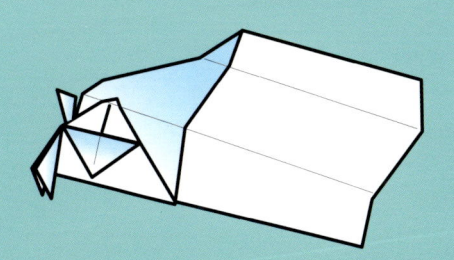

FLYING SAUCERS

Moon Scout

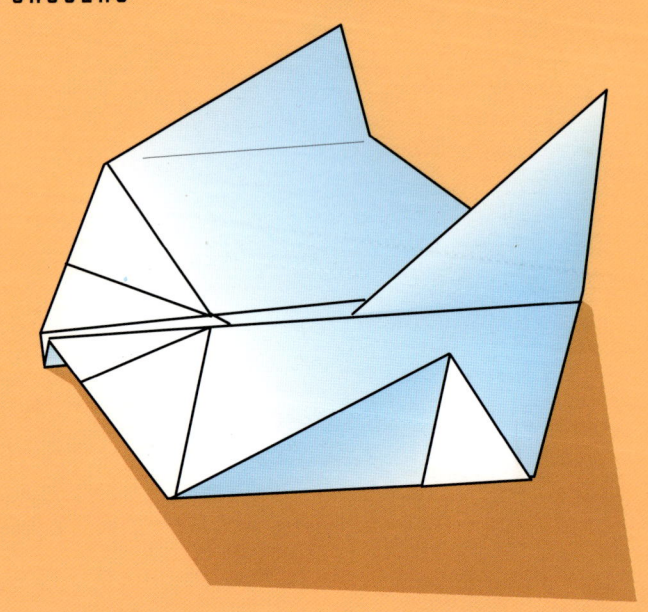

Design by Nick Robinson

This is a nippy little craft, designed for getting around your chosen planet as quickly as possible. It has many acrobatic skills if you launch it quickly. Start with a slightly larger square than usual, until you have mastered the folding method.

1 Start with a square, coloured side towards you. Fold both diagonals.

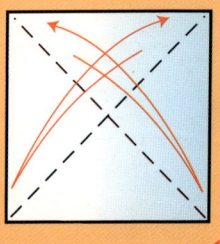

MOON SCOUT

2 Turn the paper over and fold side to side both ways.

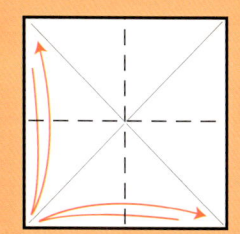

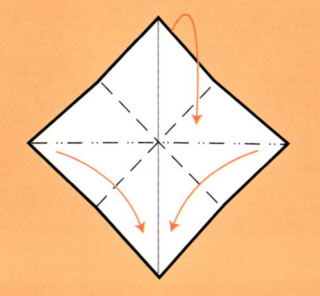

3 Using the three creases shown, bring the three furthest corners towards you. All three corners end up meeting at the nearest corner.

4 This is called a 'preliminary base'. Fold the nearest flap upwards in half.

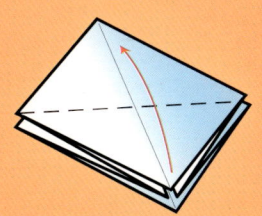

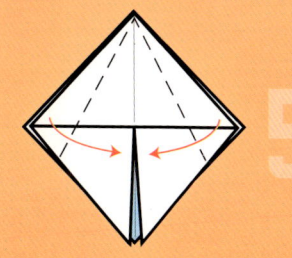

5 Fold the first layer of the two upper edges in about one-third of the way. Use the next picture as a guide.

FLYING SAUCERS

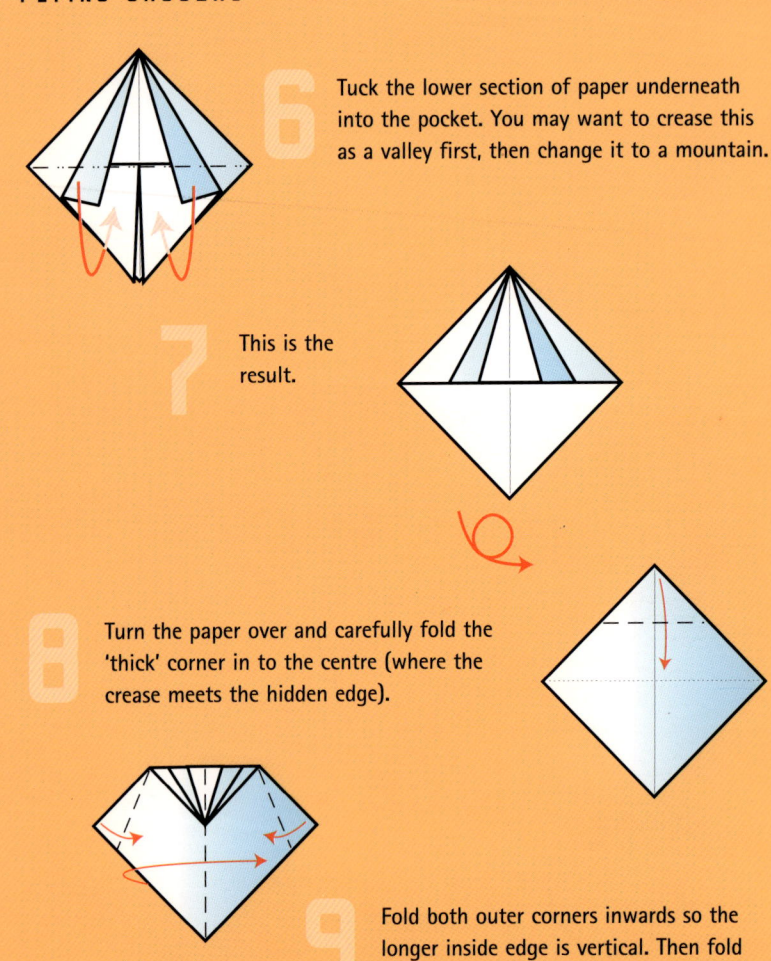

6 Tuck the lower section of paper underneath into the pocket. You may want to crease this as a valley first, then change it to a mountain.

7 This is the result.

8 Turn the paper over and carefully fold the 'thick' corner in to the centre (where the crease meets the hidden edge).

9 Fold both outer corners inwards so the longer inside edge is vertical. Then fold the paper in half from left to right.

MOON SCOUT

10 Crease both wings along the inside coloured edge.

11 Make a pre-crease as shown.

12 Push the paper in between the two layers using the crease you made in the last step.

13 Open both wings and adjust them to match the final drawing for the completed Moon Scout.

53

FLYING SAUCERS

Comet

Design by Nick Robinson
Based on an idea by Vladimir Chernov

There are many comets flying around the universe, perhaps the most famous of which is Halley's Comet. Here's a chance to make your own comet and name it after yourself! The shape of the paper and exact position of the creases are not important – experiment with both. Try to find some brightly coloured paper.

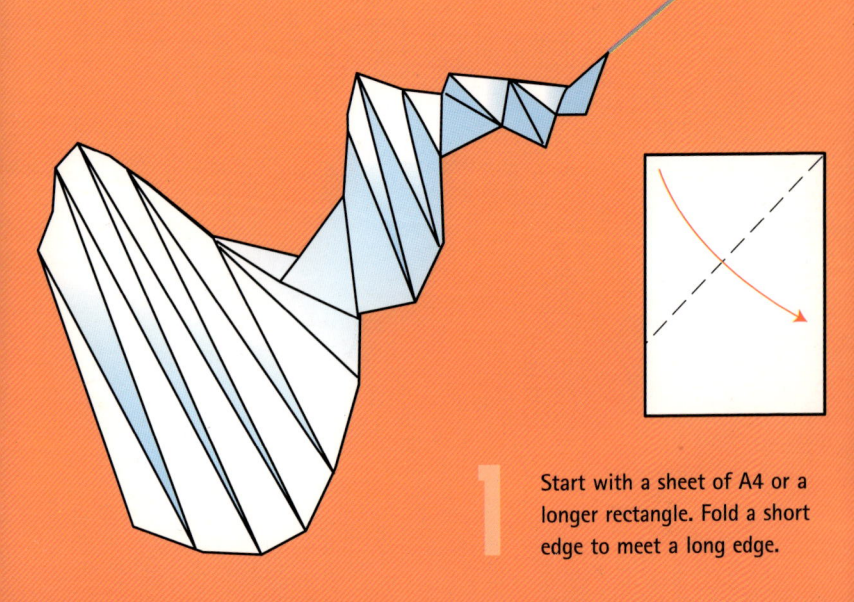

1 Start with a sheet of A4 or a longer rectangle. Fold a short edge to meet a long edge.

54

COMET

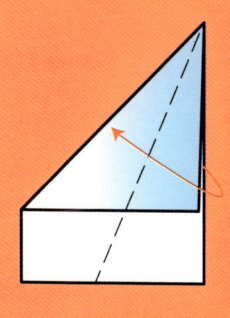

2 Take the two edges back to the folded edge.

3 Lightly crease the centre of the paper, for guidance only.

4 Fold in half, crease and unfold.

5 Now fold the end of the long crease in to the centre point. Note that the creases meet at the centre, not the large corner.

55

FLYING SAUCERS

6 Fold upper and lower edges to the centre, crease firmly and unfold. This makes the quarter creases.

7 Repeat to add the outside eighth creases.

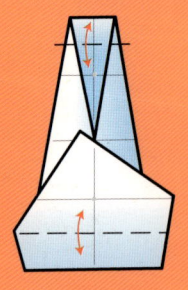

8 Fold the short edges to the opposite quarter creases to add the last eighth creases. Unfold the two flaps.

9 Now carefully add the following creases. If you hold the paper in the air, then mountain creases can be folded. On the table, you need to turn over and fold valley creases.

COMET

10 Make sure all the creases made in steps 4–8 are valley creases, then starting at the blunter corner, fold the mountain/valley creases in order.

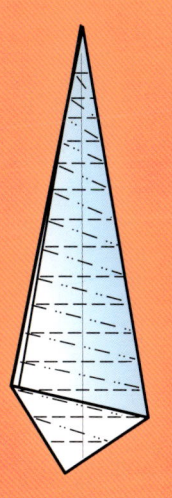

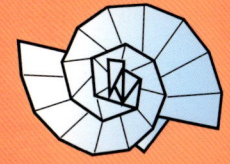

11 The paper twists into this shape.

12 Let the creases unfold slightly, then add a thread to the sharp corner. Hold the comet by this thread and run around the room!

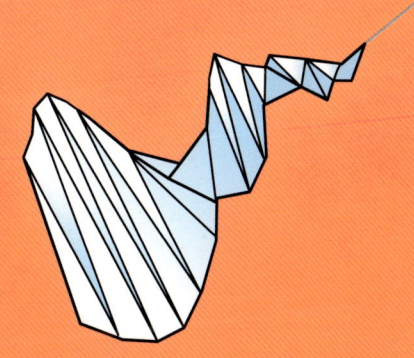

57

FLYING SAUCERS

Star Fighter

Design by Robert Neale

This sleek and elegant rocket will travel very quickly because it has a streamlined design. Ideal for repelling invading aliens, since flying saucers are often slower than Earth spacecraft. Try to find some metallic foil to make this design with.

1 Start with a preliminary base (step 4 of the Moon Scout). Turn so the four original corners are towards you, then fold the lower outer edges to the centre.

2 Fold the top triangle over the edges, crease and unfold. Open out back to a square, white side upwards.

STAR FIGHTER

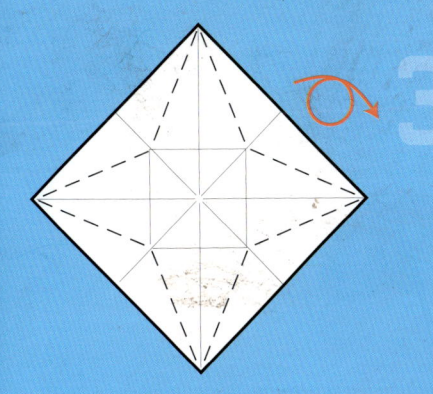

Change the creases shown into valley folds. Some will already be valleys. Turn the paper back over.

Reinforce the central square of creases, extending them to the edges of the paper.

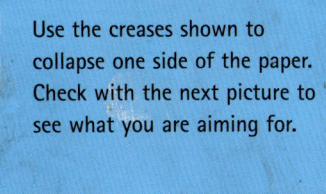

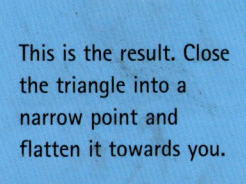

Use the creases shown to collapse one side of the paper. Check with the next picture to see what you are aiming for.

This is the result. Close the triangle into a narrow point and flatten it towards you.

59

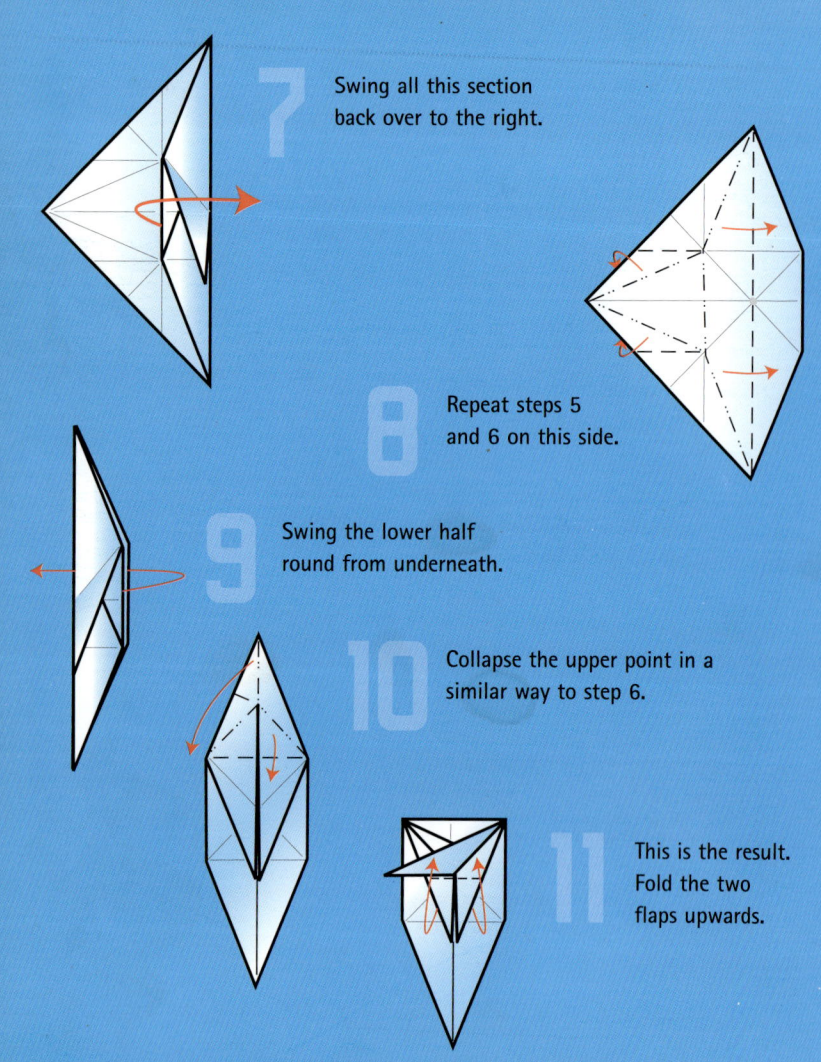

FLYING SAUCERS

7 Swing all this section back over to the right.

8 Repeat steps 5 and 6 on this side.

9 Swing the lower half round from underneath.

10 Collapse the upper point in a similar way to step 6.

11 This is the result. Fold the two flaps upwards.

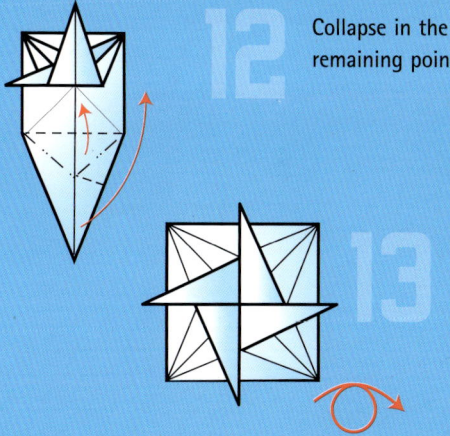

STAR FIGHTER

12 Collapse in the remaining point.

13 Rearrange one of the flaps so it points downwards, then turn the paper over.

14 Fold all the corners together using the creases shown. This move is like step 3 of the preliminary base (see Moon Scout). The model becomes three dimensional.

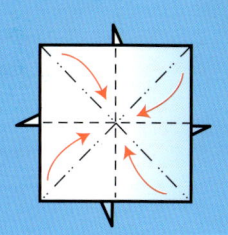

15 Fold the upper flaps over the long edges of the four points, then tuck this flap inside the pocket of the point. Repeat with the other three points.

61

FLYING SAUCERS

Glossary

Area 51 A nuclear test site in the Nevada desert, where the US government allegedly studies secret evidence about UFOs.

ASAT (Anti-Satellite) ASAT missions are where orbiting satellites are attacked.

Astronomy The study of stars, including distant galaxies and our own Sun.

Cattle mutilations Cattle have been killed, and their bodies drained of blood and mutilated, supposedly by aliens.

Crop circles Strange shapes formed by crushed grass or wheat, which have appeared in fields around the world.

Earth Resources mission Collect information about the Earth's atmosphere, land and oceans for scientific study.

Flying saucer In 1947 nine UFO sightings were reported over North West America. These were called 'flying saucers' and the name has been used ever since.

Foo fighters Strange shiny lights that followed aircraft during the Second World War.

GEO Geosynchronous orbit. A satellite in orbit in a fixed position above the Earth, which is used for communications satellites.

Hypnotic regression Some people believe that you store everything you see and hear in the subconscious memory. Using hypnosis, it is possible to relive those experiences, such as close encounters.

LEO Low Earth Orbit, below 3,000 km. Most satellites are in Low Earth Orbit.

Lunar mission These gather information about the Moon.

Lunar orbit Where the spaceship goes into orbit about the Moon.

Mars orbit Where the spaceship goes into orbit about Mars. Other planets have their own orbits.

Men In Black These people dress in black suits and travel around trying to keep alien witnesses quiet.

MEO Medium Earth Orbit. Orbits having apogees (a heavenly body's point of greatest distance from Earth) above 3,000 km, but below 30,000 km.

NASA National Aeronautics and Space Administration.

NiCd Nickel Cadmium is a type of rechargeable battery used in spaceships.

NORAD North American Aerospace Defence Command, established to protect North America from air attack. Every year approximately 25,000 UFO sightings are reported to NORAD.

Planetary mission These leave the Earth to study other planets, asteroids, and comets.

Roswell An incident alleged to have taken place in 1947 at the military base of Roswell, New Mexico. It is claimed that a flying saucer crashed during a thunderstorm, and that the army destroyed all traces of the dead aliens and the wreckage of their spacecraft. The American Government has always denied the story.

SETI Search for Extra-Terrestrial Intelligence. A US Government-funded project that monitors space, listening for messages from aliens.

Solar orbit Where the spaceship goes into orbit about the Sun.

Space stations Large orbiting structures that can support manned operations for long periods of time.

UFO Abbreviation for 'Unidentified Flying Object'. Also called flying saucers.

UFOlogy The study of UFOs.

FLYING SAUCERS

Index

A
'Absolute ceiling', 8
Air, 8, 9
Alien Lander, 30-1
Aliens, 14-19
Angle of launch, 24
Apollo Missions, 7, 10, 11
Area 51, 16
Armstrong, Neil, 7
Asteroids, 4, 12
Astronauts, 12
Atmosphere, Earth's, 8, 9, 10, 12

C
Cattle mutilations, 18
Combustion gases, 9
Comet, 54-7
Coolant, 9
Crop circles, 16

D
Dihedral, 24-5
Drag, 9

E
Escape Pod, 28
Escape velocity, 9-10

F
Flying saucers, 14-19, 36-7
Folding technique, 23
Fuel, rockets, 9

G
Gagarin, Yuri, 7
Gases, combustion, 9
Goddard, Robert, 6, 20
Gravity, 9-10, 12

L
Launch, angle of, 24
Lunar Probe, 32-3

M
Mars, 4, 7, 19
Martian bats, 42-9
Milky Way, 4
Mobiles, 38-9
Moon, 4, 7
Moon Scout, 50-3

N
NASA, 10
Newton's Laws of Motion, 8

O
Orbits, 11
Origami, 23

P
Paper-folding, 22-5
Payload, 10
Plan 9, 40-1
Propellants, 9

R
Re-entry, 12
Retro rockets, 10
Rockets, 5, 6, 8-11, 20
Roswell Incident, 17

S
Satellites, 5, 11
Space Seed, 29
Space Shuttle, 5, 7, 10, 12, 13, 34-5
Space stations, 7, 12
Speed, escape velocity, 10
Star Fighter, 58-61
Symbols, paper-folding, 23-4

T
Thrusters, 10

U
UFOs, 14-19
Universe, 4

V
V2 rockets, 6
Venus, 4
Von Braun, Werner, 6

W
Weightlessness, 12
Wings, dihedral, 24-5

FLYING SAUCERS

Acknowledgements

Thanks go to my origami friends who have encouraged me over the years, including David Brill, Wayne Brown, David Mitchell, Paul Jackson, John Smith, Kunihiko Kasahara, Philip Noble, Edwin Corrie, Alex Bateman, Paulo Mulatinho and Silke Schroeder, Mark Kennedy, Vicente Palacios, Penny Groom and many others too numerous to mention.

No thanks would be complete without mention of my patient wife Alison, son Nick jnr and shopaholic daughter Daisy.

If you have enjoyed this book, please contact the British Origami Society via:

Penny Groom
2a The Chestnuts
Countesthorpe
Leicester
LE18 3TL

The author

Nick Robinson is a former professional origami teacher, who has visited schools, libraries, youth clubs, hospitals and many other venues spreading the art of origami.

He currently scrapes a living as a computer lecturer and website designer. He has been a member of the British Origami Society for 15 years and is a serving member of its council. He writes and maintains the BOS website (www.rpmrecords.co.uk/bos).

Nick has promoted origami on the television, radio and Internet. His original designs have been published around the world and he has written several books on the subject, including an entry for the *Encarta Encyclopedia*. A former professional musician, he performs live concerts of improvised, ambient guitar and gigs with band Satsuma! His website can be found at: www.cheesypeas.demon.co.uk.